THE MASTER OF THE WORLD

JULES VERNE

CAMPFIRE™

KALYANI NAVYUG MEDIA PVT LTD
New Delhi

Sitting around the Campfire, telling the story, were:

Wordsmith	:	Dale Mettam
Illustrator	:	Suresh Digwal
Colourist	:	Pradeep Sherawat
Colour Consultant	:	RC Prakash
Letterer	:	Bhavnath Chaudhary
Editors	:	Suparna Deb
		Eman Chowdhary

Cover Artists:

Illustrator	:	Suresh Digwal
Colourist	:	Jayakrishnan K P
Designer	:	Jayakrishnan K P

Published by Kalyani Navyug Media Pvt Ltd
101 C, Shiv House, Hari Nagar Ashram
New Delhi 110014
India
www.campfire.co.in

ISBN: 978-81-906963-4-0

Printed in India at Rave India

About The Author

Jules Gabriel Verne was born in Nantes, France on 8th February 1828. Over the following 77 years, he became both a prodigious writer and a creator of characters that would be known throughout the world. His work continues to live on well beyond his death, and he is known by many as the father of modern science fiction.

Sent to Paris to study law, like his father before him, Verne soon discovered that his real talent lay in writing. This gift established him as an author of exciting and extravagant adventures. Sometimes these stories revolved around the use of technologies of the day, such as in his novels *Five Days in a Balloon* and *Around the World in Eighty Days*. However, what made Verne really stand out were the flights of fancy he took with regard to the potential advances in technology. His fantastic creations were based, in many respects, on a keen understanding of science and the way it was moving forward.

In France, Verne was greatly encouraged to pursue his writing talent when he met Alexandre Dumas, the famous author. Verne produced several plays between 1851 and 1861 and, during that time, met and married Honorine Fraysse. In the years that followed, he began to concentrate on novels, and the first of his better known books was published in 1864 – *A Journey to the Centre of the Earth*.

Predicting such revolutionary concepts as gas-powered automobiles, skyscrapers, submarines, journeys to the moon and high-speed trains, Verne truly laid the groundwork for his belief that 'whatever one man is capable of conceiving, other men will be able to achieve'. He also correctly predicted that developments in technology would one day lead to the production of weapons of mass destruction.

Verne died on 24th March 1905. Whatever reasons someone has for reading his works, one thing is assured: while his stories about the future range from frighteningly accurate to wildly speculative, his novels provide an entertaining adventure based in a world that is not that distant from our own, but is intriguing, dangerous and thrilling.

John Strock

Commissioner Ward

Robur

Elias Smith

I have always felt the strong desire to investigate and understand everything which is mysterious. So, as head inspector in the federal police department at Washington, I became very interested in these remarkable occurrences.

Yet, what I initially thought was a waste of my time, proved to be one of the most curious and dangerous cases I have ever investigated.

It's hard to believe how this one incident, on this one night, would create such chaos in my life.

If I hadn't witnessed the events with my own eyes, I wouldn't have believed them myself. Yet, everything you're about to read is true.

6

Deep amongst the Blueridge Mountains rises the summit known as the Great Eyrie. Its huge form can be distinctly seen from the little town of Morganton on the Catawba River.

The Great Eyrie appears rocky and grim and inaccessible and, on certain days, it has a strange blue and distant effect.

It was from this mountain that rumblings began to be heard. They were accompanied by heavy clouds and flickering lights at night. And people began to realise that the Great Eyrie was a serious source of danger.

On 25th April, I was called to the office of Commissioner Ward.

Come in, Strock.

Are you as fond of riddles as ever? As eager to penetrate into mysteries as I have known you before?

I am, Mr Ward.

I'm sure you've read about that fuss down in North Carolina, Strock. It's been in all the newspapers of late.

The volcano near Morganton, sir? It would arouse anyone's curiosity. What about it?

You'll be investigating it, Strock. That's what.

Bu--

But it's a waste of your time? Sit down, Strock. Let me explain.

The day after the explosions that terrified the locals, a man with one of those hot-air balloons was in the area.

The local mayor asked this man to go up and see what he could see. Everything was going well, but then the wind took a turn and pushed the balloon in the wrong direction.

Wouldn't this be more of a case for a scientist? I'm sure there are some geologists at the Smithsonian who would leap at the chance to investigate this.

8

You will be assigned to the Mayor of Morganton, who will assist you. Be prudent, Strock, and tell no one about your mission unless it is absolutely necessary.

WOO-CHUG-CHUG-CHUG-CHUG

And so I had begun that fateful investigation.

Soon I was on a train, heading south to discover the mystery of the Great Eyrie.

The information gathered so far was slim, leaving me a long and tedious journey to endure.

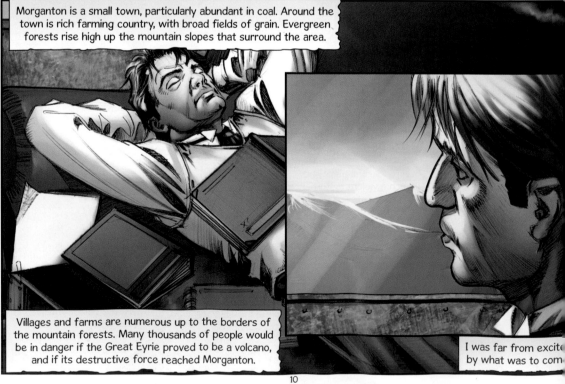

Morganton is a small town, particularly abundant in coal. Around the town is rich farming country, with broad fields of grain. Evergreen forests rise high up the mountain slopes that surround the area.

Villages and farms are numerous up to the borders of the mountain forests. Many thousands of people would be in danger if the Great Eyrie proved to be a volcano, and if its destructive force reached Morganton.

I was far from excite by what was to com

Elias Smith, the Mayor of Morganton, had been informed of my arrival by Commissioner Ward.

He was vigorous and enterprising, at least forty years of age, and in the peak of health

I was welcomed into his home, where he quickly briefed me on the situation.

So, at Washington they wish to know what the Great Eyrie has hidden inside?

Yes, Mr Smith.

My family has been in this area for many years and I don't know of a natural event which co cause what I witnessed several nights a And I must confess that this mystery intrigues me greatly.

I don't know if it was the new day dawning, or the fact that I had a new mystery to finally sink my teeth into...

...but the next morning, I was filled with renewed determination. Mayor Smith had hired the services of two local guides and we set out to explore the Great Eyrie.

We left Morganton by a road which wound along the left bank of the Catawba River. The day was beautiful, and the fresh air was cool, like a perfect April morning.

It was a one day trek to the foot of the Great Eyrie, where we decided to camp.

Although tired after the day's hike, I was determined to pursue our quest to the end.

My chief has instructed me to snatch the secret from this demon of the Great Eyrie.

We will snatch it from him, Mr Strock, whether he likes it or not even if we have to search the bowels of the mountain.

At length, we debated what we might find inside this great mountain. But I must confess, at that point of the investigation, I had formed no opinion.

14

The next morning, the two guides went ahead to find the most practical paths for us to take. Elias Smith and I followed at a more leisurely pace.

We walked by a narrow gorge amongst rocks and trees. A tiny stream trickled downwards under our feet.

It became evident that the ascent of the Great Eyrie would take far more time than we had originally estimated. Now we could only go ahead blindly, and trust the instincts of our two guides.

My wife was not too happy about me bringing you gents up here, you know.

Why not?

The word in town is that the Devil himself has taken up residence on the Great Eyrie.

And so, gentlemen, tomorrow we will solve the mystery that has plagued our fair town.

An hour later, our route was blocked. To the right and the left grew impenetrable masses of trees and bushes. It would have been easier to scale cliffs than pass through these.

We now needed to decide where we should turn for a new route.

I suggest we turn in now, gentlemen. We have a long climb ahead of us tomorrow.

Having made many attempts to find a more practical path, we all agreed that a rest would refresh us.

By the middle of the next morning, we were at the rock face. I must admit I was possessed by the demon of curiosity.

The Great Eyrie took on an absolutely fantastic appearance. It seemed to be populated by dragons and huge monsters. If creatures from mythology had appeared to guard it, I would not have been surprised.

At first glance, climbing it seemed an impossible task. But the rocks were craggy and provided excellent foot and handholds.

It reminded me of my youth when I would go on similar rock climbing adventures. And slowly I began to enjoy this investigation.

But, as would become the pattern of this entire story, as soon as I overcame one obstacle...

...another would leap up to take its place.

If I returned without even getting to the top of the mountain, my mission would have been a complete failure.

A profound silence reigned around us, and a perfectly clear sky shone overhead. We experienced the perfect calm of great altitudes.

We calculated that the circumference of the huge wall was about 1,200 or 1,500 feet. As for the space inside, we could not comprehend that without knowing the thickness of the wall.

The surroundings were absolutely deserted. it seemed like no living creature had ever come this high, except the few birds of prey which soared above us.

Perhaps it was dislodged by the explosion.

With great difficulty, they searched for a way into the mountain.

But it seemed that nature had worked as man does, with careful regularity. There was no break in the wall; no way into this fortress.

You don't believe in the superstitions that surround the Great Eyrie then?

I am a man of science. I believe what I can prove.

Despite what the newspapers reported, there were no earthquakes that night.

And I would think, if the Devil himself were breaking free from Hell, might at least see the od ripple in my brandy as he did it.

No way up, sir.

That boulder did break free of the wall up there, but there's still no way inside.

Then we're left with one course of action.

Mayor Smith and I will go clockwise, you two go anti-clockwise, and we'll see what we find as we go around the ledge.

...ter some time, we came face ...o face with our guides again.

Nothing, sir. You?

We found nothing either.

A thousand devils! We still have no idea what is inside this confounded mountain; not even if it is a crater.

And at that moment, I knew there was no way forward. At every point there was ...lways that mighty wall, a hundred feet high!

I knew that the Great Eyrie had beaten us – had beaten me – and her secrets were still hidden deep inside her.

It pained me to abandon our effort, and descend the slope without completing my mission. I felt an urgent need to persist – my curiosity had increased.

...ut what could I do? Could I tear open the solid rocks? Leap over the mighty cliff? Throwing one last defiant glare at the Great Eyrie, I followed my companions.

We returned without much difficulty. We only had to slide down where we had so laboriously scrambled up earlier. Before five o'clock, we had reached the bottom of the mountain.

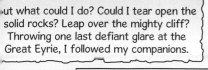

If I had known that wouldn't be the last I would see of the Great Eyrie, I might have been less disappointed.

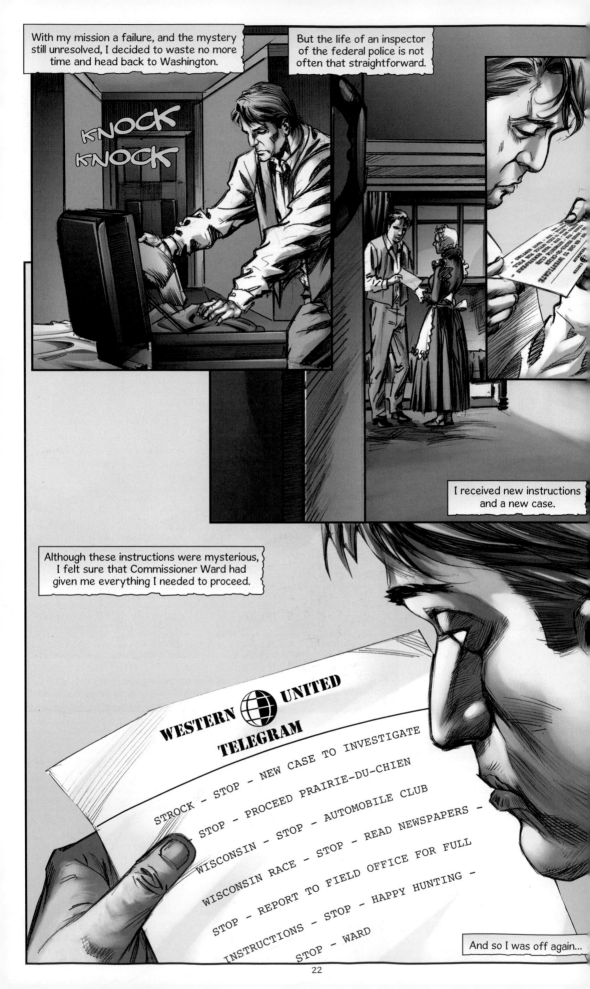

WOO-CHUG-CHUG-CHUG-CHUG-CHUG

...with no time to dwell on my failures. I had a new case to investigate, and one that I knew would be more to my liking.

Fortunately, Mayor Smith had kept all the newspapers from the last week, and I took them with me.

All were full of the same news; a mysterious automobile that was the scourge of the highways.

At that time, the most advanced cars could not reach much more than 60 miles an hour. Even the railways, with their rapid express trains, struggled to exceed this speed on the best lines of America and Europe.

This new automobile, which was astonishing the world, travelled at more than double that speed.

RICHMOND HERALD

SATAN DRIVES THROUGH VIRGINIA

The fair state of Virginia became the latest member of the Union to experience what some have named *The Devil's Automobile*. The vehicle travels at such immense speeds that some have claimed it becomes invisible to the human eye.

Panic has spread across the country recently, and the authorities have been unable to catch this hellish chauffeur, let alone discover his true identity.

Scientific expert Dr James W Giddens has

speculated that it would be incredibly dangerous for anyone and anything in the path of a vehicle travelling at such incredible speeds. Local Police have attempted to allay the fears of the

public, but these measures seem too little, too late.

'It's nonsense!' declared Mr J Kershaw. 'This madman would easily know how to circle around such obstructions as the police are proposing.'

'If necessary', said Mrs L Becker, 'the machine would leap over the barriers. And if he is indeed the Devil, he has, as a former angel, presumably preserved his wings, and would show

Contd on pg-2

No one knew who the vehicle belonged to, nor where it came from, nor where it went. Even the Devil himself had no right to travel at such speed over the roads of the United States...

...without a special permit, without a number on his car, and without a regular licence. It seemed that I was once again on the trail of the Devil, but this time I had a plan.

A race was to be held by the Automobile Club of Wisconsin. The route was about 200 miles long, starting from Prairie-du-chien and ending a little above Milwaukee on the edge of Lake Michigan.

Many machines, from various countries, had entered this great race. The 50,000 dollar prize made sure that it would be keenly contested. New records were expected to be set, and an enormous crowd had gathered.

I didn't believe for a minute that the driver of the incredible automobile that had dominated the news was anything other than human. And this would be the perfect place for him to reveal himself.

My instructions had been to catch and arrest the driver of this vehicle.

RICHMOND HERALD

What Rules the Roads?

He had broken the highway laws in several states, disturbed the peace, and proved to be an enormous embarrassment to the police of the nation.

Despite my lack of time to prepare, I'd concocted a plan I felt would do the trick.

I was confident that my failure at the Great Eyrie would soon be eclipsed by my victory here in Wisconsin.

Suddenly, at half past nine, two miles away from the starting line, a tremendous noise was heard.

LOOK!

It's the Devil's automobile!

It is that infernal machine!

At last!

The rumbling sound came from the middle of a flying cloud of dust, and was accompanied by shrieks like those of a siren.

It's just a dust storm.

No, look! It's coming this way!

Down the road!

VROOOM

The crowds hardly had time to move to one side before the cloud swept by like a hurricane.

It was moving at no less than 150 miles an hour, and no one could make out what it was.

I hadn't expected it to stop there, but I'd taken certain steps to make sure it stopped further down the road.

The ghost passed and disappeared in an instant, leaving behind it a long trail of dust.

Incredible as it seems, the vehicle had beaten my men at every stage. But I was confident that, at this point of the race, everything would go according to plan.

LOOK!

Impossible! No one should be here yet!

It's the Devil's vehicle!

Just beyond the finish line, the road curved sharply, forcing everyone to slow down or face certain death. And beyond that was Lake Michigan.

We'll all be killed!

My God!

WOOOOOOSH

It's not slowing down!

WOOOOOSH

Someone call a doctor!

Call a scrap metal dealer more like. No one could survive that!

The Devil has returned to Hades.

And so, with the apparent suicide of this insane driver, there were now two cases in a row I'd failed to solve.

But there were more strange events to come, as I would discover...

...when I returned to Washington.

FEDERAL POLICE HEADQUARTERS

Not been a good couple of weeks for you, Strock.

I can explain, sir. Th--

Nonsense, Strock. Your record is exemplary. In hindsight, I perhaps overreact to the potential threat of the Great Eyrie...

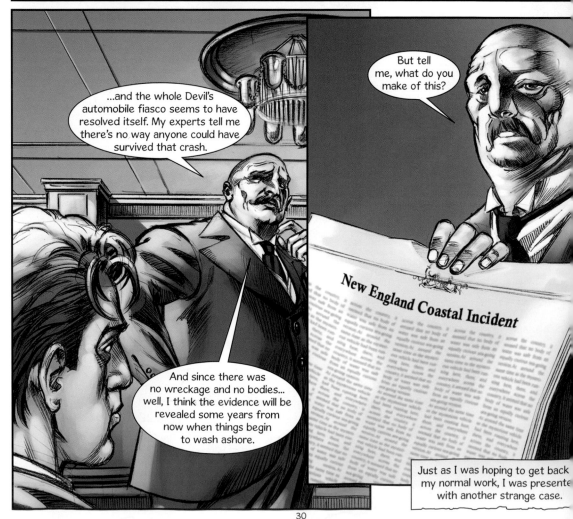

...and the whole Devil's automobile fiasco seems to have resolved itself. My experts tell me there's no way anyone could have survived that crash.

But tell me, what do you make of this?

And since there was no wreckage and no bodies... well, I think the evidence will be revealed some years from now when things begin to wash ashore.

New England Coastal Incident

Just as I was hoping to get back my normal work, I was presente with another strange case.

For some days, there had been [re]ports of an object that moved with [l]ightning speed across the water.

Some claimed that it was a sea monster of some kind. Yet its appearance and intelligence suggested it was not.

[W]henever a challenge seemed [like]ly, it would immediately change direction or speed away.

[T]here were many different opinions about what it was, but none of them were based on evidence.

If this monster was not one of those huge marine mammals, then what was it? Was it one of the legendary dwellers of the deep, like the krakens, the octopuses, the leviathans and the famous sea serpents?

Marine biologists claimed it was a never-seen-before behemoth, but its appearance in fresh water lakes, as well as oceans, seemed to dismiss this idea.

[W]hatever it was, the thing was [c]ausing the same kind of panic and fear on water that the [a]utomobile had caused on land.

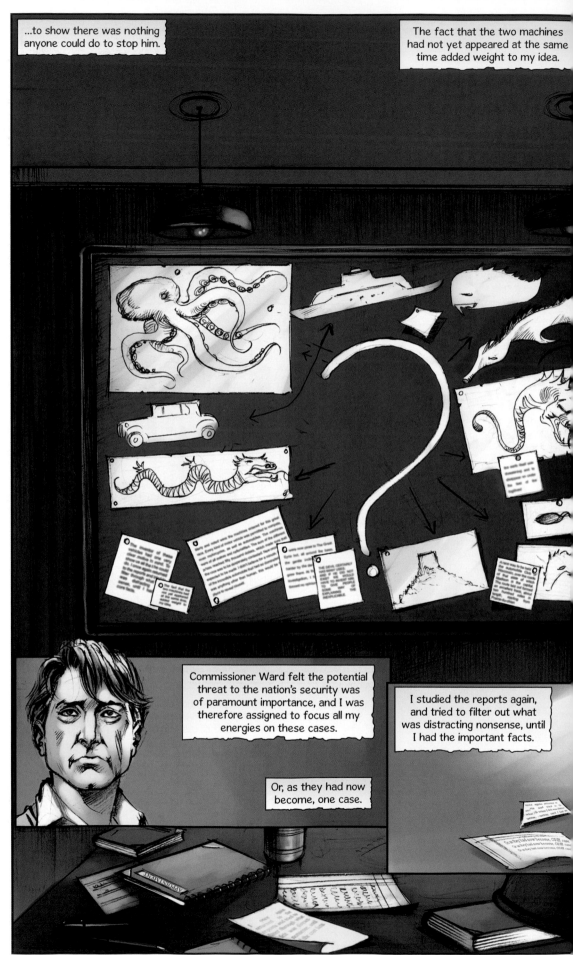

...to show there was nothing anyone could do to stop him.

The fact that the two machines had not yet appeared at the same time added weight to my idea.

Commissioner Ward felt the potential threat to the nation's security was of paramount importance, and I was therefore assigned to focus all my energies on these cases.

I studied the reports again, and tried to filter out what was distracting nonsense, until I had the important facts.

Or, as they had now become, one case.

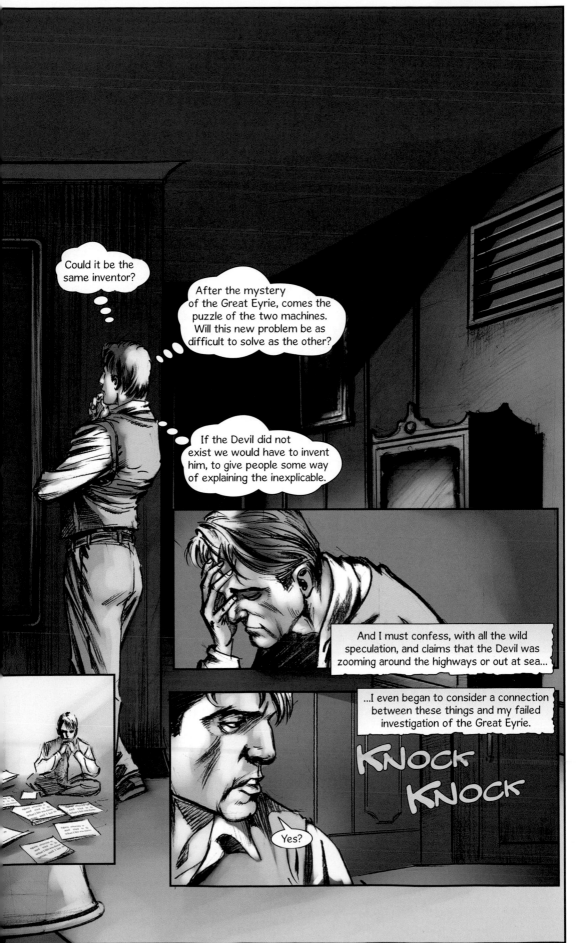

There was no signature! Nothing but three initials at the end of the last line.

But, while my guess about the subject of the letter was correct...

Great Eyrie, Blueridge Mtns, North Carolina, June 13.

To Mr Strock
Chief Inspector of Police
34 Long St, Washington DC

Sir,
You were charged with the mission of penetrating the Great Eyrie.
You came on April the twenty-eighth, accompanied by the Mayor of Morganton and two guides. You mounted to the foot of the wall, and you encircled it, finding it too high and steep to climb. You sought a breech and you found none. Know this: none enter the Great Eyrie; or if one enters, he never returns. Do not try again, for the second attempt will not result as did the first, but will have grave consequences for you.

Heed this warning, or evil fortune will come to you.

M. O. W

...the sendor was most definitely not Mayor Smith.

A joke, without doubt.

Why had that letter come then, when I'd almost forgotten my expedition to the Great Eyrie, and when I was involved in a new case that was much more important?

Then, as quickly as this insanity around the country began, it ended.

There was no news from Morganton. Everything seemed to have returned to sleepy normality.

The roads of Wisconsin saw no more of that mysterious automobile. Nor did the rest of the country.

If the daring driver had not died, then he must have left America.

And the waters off New England were once again free from the talk of monsters, leaving the fishermen to return to their usual complaints, and the tourists to their cruises.

Nothing led me to think that I would leave Washington any time soon, though in my line of duty you can never be certain about what tomorrow holds.

Then a curious thing happened

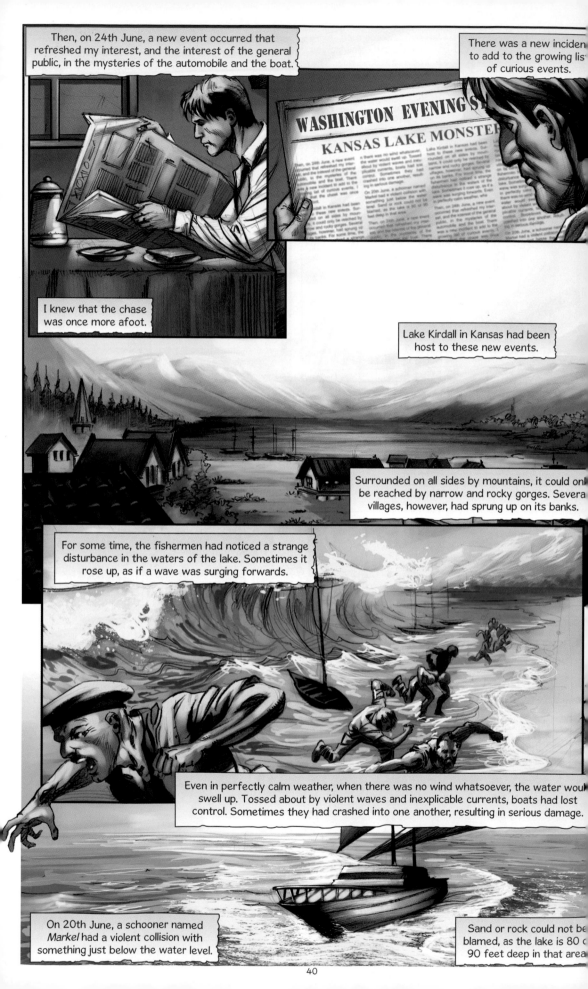

Then, on 24th June, a new event occurred that refreshed my interest, and the interest of the general public, in the mysteries of the automobile and the boat.

There was a new incident to add to the growing list of curious events.

WASHINGTON EVENING ST

KANSAS LAKE MONSTER

I knew that the chase was once more afoot.

Lake Kirdall in Kansas had been host to these new events.

Surrounded on all sides by mountains, it could only be reached by narrow and rocky gorges. Several villages, however, had sprung up on its banks.

For some time, the fishermen had noticed a strange disturbance in the waters of the lake. Sometimes it rose up, as if a wave was surging forwards.

Even in perfectly calm weather, when there was no wind whatsoever, the water would swell up. Tossed about by violent waves and inexplicable currents, boats had lost control. Sometimes they had crashed into one another, resulting in serious damage.

On 20th June, a schooner named *Markel* had a violent collision with something just below the water level.

Sand or rock could not be blamed, as the lake is 80 or 90 feet deep in that area.

40

The Captain, an experienced man, was stunned by the incident...

...and with the schooner badly damaged, it was in great danger of sinking.

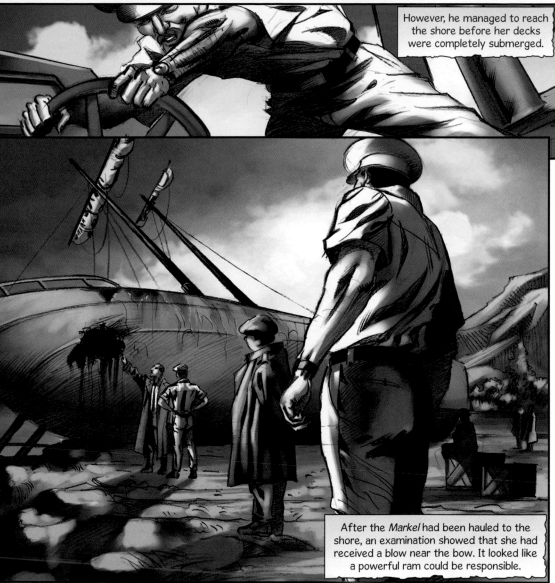

However, he managed to reach the shore before her decks were completely submerged.

After the *Markel* had been hauled to the shore, an examination showed that she had received a blow near the bow. It looked like a powerful ram could be responsible.

SUBMARIN

From this it seems evident that there is a submarine beneath the surface of Lake Kirdall which moves about with amazing speed.

42

You, Strock! You will catch this man and arrest him.

All agents of the federal police force have been notified.

On what grounds, sir?

I have drawn up this special arrest warrant.

You must be ready to leave Washington at any moment. Whatever you do, do not lose sight of him.

The charge is a threat to the security of this nation and its citizens.

You can count on me, Mr Ward. At any hour, day or night, I shall be ready. Thank you for trusting me with this mission. If it succeeds, it will be a great honour.

As I walked home, I felt less confident than Commissioner Ward.

I prepared everything for a trip of unknown duration. Perhaps Mrs Fogg thought I was planning a return to the Great Eyrie, but she said nothing.

As sure as I was of her discretion, I told her nothing. I would confide in no one about this great mission.

Several days passed without news of the automobile, the boat or the submarine. There were plenty of rumours, but the police knew they were all false.

Conflicting reports came in. One day, the automobile was spotted heading north through Arkansas.

Then, just hours later, the mysterious vehicle was seen surging across Lake Superior.

Even if the automobile could have travelled at such an incredible speed, how could it have crossed the whole country without being seen?

While there could be two vehicles, the man behind them could not be in both places at once.

After these two brief appearances, if they were actually appearances, the machine vanished again.

And I was left thinking that these reports did more to harm my investigation than help it.

An official notice was published in every newspaper of the United States on 3rd July.

THE NEW YORK TIMES

NOTICE

During the month of April, of the present year, an automobile traversed the roads of Pennsylvania, of Kentucky, of Ohio, of Tennessee, of Missouri, of Illinois; and on the 27th of May, during the race held by the American Automobile Club, it covered the course in Wisconsin. Then it disappeared.

During the first week of June, a boat manoeuvring at great speed appeared off the coast of New England, between Cape Cod and Cape Sable, and more particularly, around Boston. Then it disappeared.

In the second fortnight of the same month, a submarine boat was run beneath the waters of Lake Kirdall, in Kansas. Then it disappeared.

Everything points to the belief that the same inventor must have built these three machines, or perhaps that they are the same machine, constructed so as to travel both on land and in water.

A proposition is therefore addressed to the said inventor, whoever he be, with the aim of acquiring the said machines.

He is requested to make himself known and to name the terms upon which he will deal with the United States government. He is also requested to answer as promptly as possible to the Department of Federal Police, Washington DC, United States of America.

I didn't know if this was a piece of cheese set in a trap to aid my cause, or if the powers above me really intended to offer this man an unlimited reward for his invention.

It would surely be worth a great deal to the government, if they got hold of it.

The day passed. There came no answer, no letter, no telegram!

Other nations of the world also hoped to obtain possession of the wonderful invention. Several governments made equally tempting offers.

Time passed. There was no further news of our man. There was no response from him. He appeared no more.

But then, on 15th July, a response was received.

45

The letter was addressed to the government of the United States.

KNOCK KNOCK

Is there any news, sir?

Enter.

Indeed. Although not the kind we'd hoped for. Take a look yourself, Strock.

Instead of sending it by post, our man had come to Washington and deposited it himself. But no one had seen who had placed it in the police mailbox.

On Board The Terror, 15th July.

To the Old and New World,

The propositions emanating from the different governments of Europe, in addition to that which has finally been made by the United States of America, need expect no other answer than this:
I refuse absolutely and definitely the sums offered for my invention. My machine will be neither French nor German, nor Austrian nor Russian, nor English nor American.
The invention will remain my own, and I shall use it as pleases me. With it, I hold control of the entire world, and there lies no force within the reach of humanity which is able to resist me, under any circumstances whatsoever.
Let no one attempt to seize or stop me. It is, and will be, utterly impossible. Whatever injury anyone attempts against me, I will return a hundredfold.
As to the money which is offered me, I despise it! I have no need of it. Moreover, on the day when it pleases me to have millions, or billions, I have but to reach out my hand and take them.
Let both the Old and the New World realise this: They can accomplish nothing against me; I can accomplish anything against them.

I sign this letter:
The Master of the World.

The nerve of the scoundrel!

What is it, Strock? You look like you've seen a ghost.

In a way, perhaps I have. Or rather, less of a ghost and more of a mysterious phantom.

Judge for yourself.

So the mysterious inventor had reappeared in the United States! He had not crossed the Atlantic and, if we were to capture him now, it would probably be in Ohio – the state in which Toledo is situated.

And so I was off again, Though this time I was fille with renewed enthusiasm.

WOO-CHU-CHUG-CHUG-CHUG

Would I finally catch this man who'd plagued me so much in recent weeks?

The following morning, I arrived and was met by Agent Wells. He'd seen the vehicle we now called the *Terror* and had arranged for our transportation.

Are we going to stop in Toledo?

Mr Strock?

Yes.

No. With your permission, Mr Strock, we must leave at once to reach our destination. We have to get to Black Rock Creek, which is twenty miles away.

I am at your command.

Arthur Wells was one of the best of our local police agents. Cool in danger and always enterprising, he had proven his bravery on more than one occasion while risking his life.

By mid-afternoon, we arrived at Black Rock Creek.

BLACK ROCK CREEK 1 MILE

The surface of Lake Erie covers about 10,000 square miles and receives its water from the greater lakes to the west. At its northeastern end it empties into Lake Ontario via the Niagara River and its famous waterfalls.

Our carriage followed a rough and rarely used road along the border of the lake. As we went along, Art Wells told me what he had learnt.

From across the lake he had seen a submarine rise up suddenly and stop at the mouth of Black Rock Creek. When the submarine was close to the rocks, two men climbed out. He was alone on the edge of the creek, otherwise he would have definitely captured them.

How much further?

Just through those woods. We can leave the horses and trap here, and sneak down to the water's edge.

And you've seen them here?

The past two nights, Mr Strock, sir.

I say we squat down and wait, sir. They've arrived at around dusk the last two nights.

Very well.

Nearly an hour passed by. We could not bring ourselves to leave the place, and our eyes tried to see through the darkness.

Sometimes we thought we saw a shadow outlined against the dark; the silhouette of an approaching boat.

But they all disappeared one after the other. They were just illusions created by our minds.

Do you hear that?

They're coming, sir!

And then, the waters swelled up at the foot of the rocks and caught our attention.

Silent, motionless, we strained our eyes and ears.

The disturbance seemed to be caused by a boat, either from beneath the water, or approaching the creek on the lake.

At last!

I leaned close to the water to watch the movement. It started to become more evident, and I began to notice a sort of regular throbbing.

A boat is definitely coming towards us.

Yes. Is this where you saw the boat before?

Yes, just here.

We could just about see a black mass moving through the darkness. It advanced very slowly, and we could hardly hear the faint noise of its engines.

Almost no sound at all, Wells.

Indeed, sir.

Electrically powered, I bet.

It seemed that this was the submarine which Wells had seen previously, and it was returning to spend the night within the shelter of the creek.

I'm going in.

I left our hiding place, and made my way to the quay.

There were no lights on the deck. Not a single ray came from within the cabin.

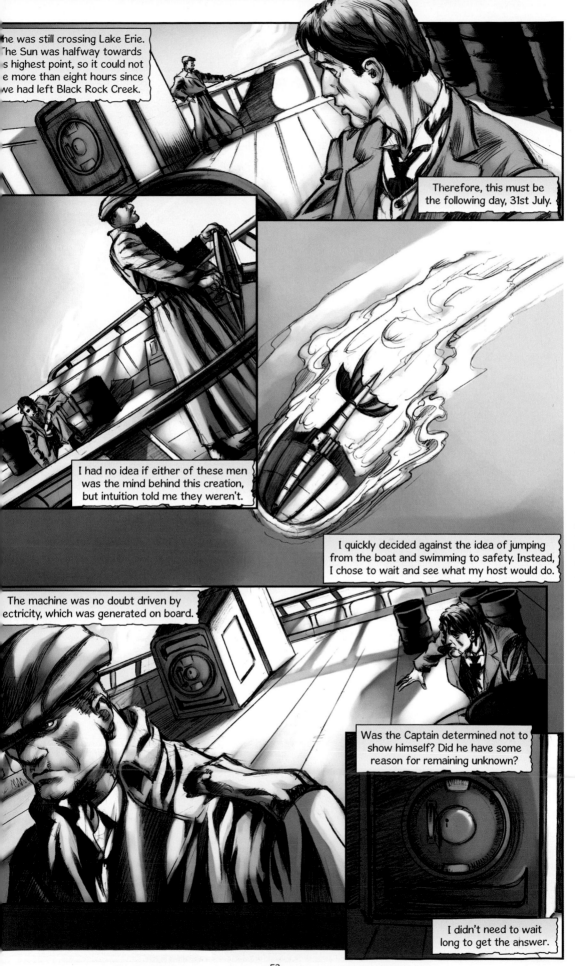

The man I had so impatiently waited for finally appeared on deck. The Captain, having scanned the horizon, checked his compass, and instructed our course to be altered slightly.

Are you the Captain?

He said nothing.

Is this the *Terror*?

Again, nothing.

What do you plan to do with me?

Words seemed ready to burst from his lips but he held them back with visible irritation. His hand touched a regulator of some sort and the *Terror* rapidly increased its speed

Hours passed, but the situation did not change. Suddenly there was a tremor...

...and, as I looked around, I saw that two torpedo destroyers had moved in and were pursuing us.

These destroyers were the quickest boats in the country, driven by powerful engines using the most modern technology.

We now stand between those destroyers and Niagara Falls!

Pah!

Our captain took the helm. One of his men was at the bow, and the other in the engine room.

The Master of the World showed complete disdain towards these boats. He seemed to believe that the destroyers were powerless against him.

BADOOM

BADOOM

About a mile separated us from the two powerful fighters. Our captain permitted them to approach closer still. Then he pressed a handle down.

BLOOOSH

BLOOOSH

The *Terror*, doubling the speed of her propellers, leapt across the surface of the lake. She played with the destroyers! Instead of turning to escape, she continued moving forwards.

Cannon shots boomed above us.

BA-DOOOOM

I glanced around anxiously. The Captain did not even turn his head; and I shall never forget the expression of pure hate on his face.

BLOOOSH

The *Terror* might be able to avoid the shots of the destroyers, but we were going nowhere; we were heading towards Niagara Falls.

So, now what would this Master of the World do?

Presumably he would change his course, unless he preferred to speed to the land and continue his route along the roads.

BADOOM

We were now less than half a mile ahead of the destroyers, which were pursuing us at top speed.

The lake had narrowed and there was no way back. We were trapped, and the only way forwards was over Niagara Falls.

The famous falls, in the middle of this great river, are over 150 feet high.

No matter how perfect this machine was, it could not escape the power of the great falls. We seemed doomed.

Suddenly, a sharp noise was heard from the machinery within the craft, and...

...at the moment when the *Terror* reached the very edge of the falls, she arose into space!

It could **fly**! In addition to commanding the roads and the seas...

...my captor was also a master of the heavens!

Perhaps, the inventor of such a vehicle **WAS** the Master of the World!

The machine moved through the air like a bird, with its huge wings beating with tremendous power!

Perhaps his letters had not been boastful after all.

Just as the *Terror* rose above the Canadian Falls, the clear evening allowed me to notice the direction in which we were travelling.

This machine actually had four uses! It was an automobile, a boat, a submarine and an airship. Earth, sea and air...

...it could move through all three elements! And with what power! With what speed!

Half an hour after the *Terror* soared into the air, I had sunk into complete unconsciousness. I hadn't realised it was happening – I must have been drugged.

Our commander certainly did not want me to know the route he took

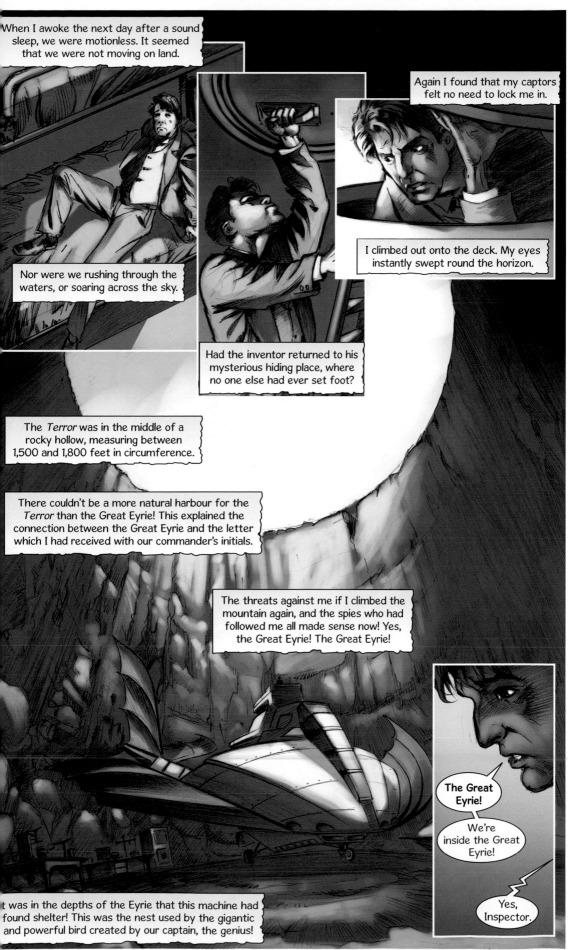

When I awoke the next day after a sound sleep, we were motionless. It seemed that we were not moving on land.

Nor were we rushing through the waters, or soaring across the sky.

Again I found that my captors felt no need to lock me in.

I climbed out onto the deck. My eyes instantly swept round the horizon.

Had the inventor returned to his mysterious hiding place, where no one else had ever set foot?

The *Terror* was in the middle of a rocky hollow, measuring between 1,500 and 1,800 feet in circumference.

There couldn't be a more natural harbour for the *Terror* than the Great Eyrie! This explained the connection between the Great Eyrie and the letter which I had received with our commander's initials.

The threats against me if I climbed the mountain again, and the spies who had followed me all made sense now! Yes, the Great Eyrie! The Great Eyrie!

The Great Eyrie!

We're inside the Great Eyrie!

Yes, Inspector.

It was in the depths of the Eyrie that this machine had found shelter! This was the nest used by the gigantic and powerful bird created by our captain, the genius!

59

Two years before the sighting of the vehicle, Robur had appeared at the Weldon Institute – a club devoted to all things aeronautical.

He had interrupted a meeting and ridiculed the Institute's plans for a lighter-than-air vehicle.

In turn, the Institute's members ridiculed his suggestion that a heavier-than-air machine would work, and mockingly named him...

Robur the Conqueror.

Robur the Conqueror.

Robur the Conqueror.

Robur the Conqueror.

One week later, surrounded by much pomp and ceremony, the Weldon Institute launched their flying ship, the *Go-Ahead*.

However, they had not counted on the arrival of Robur...

...nor the method of his appearance.

Witnesses said they didn't believe Robur, in his flying machine, The *Albatross*, was trying to destroy The *Go-Ahead*...

...but his reckless flying resulted in that happening.

Rather than let the two men aboard the doomed airship fall to their deaths, Robur swooped in and saved them...

...whisking them away to what was later referred to as the mysterious Island X.

Several days later, when Robur released his hostages unharmed, many expected further action...

...but this curious man, of great intelligence and courage, simply flew away, never to be seen again!

Until now!

Only one man could link the identity of the Master of the World with Robur the Conqueror. And that man was I, his prisoner.

You've caused me a great deal of inconvenience, Inspector Strock. Because of you, I must give up this haven.

And what are your plans for me, Robur?

I've yet to decide...

...but for now, you should stand clear of these remains.

You were using parts of the *Albatross* to build the *Terror*!

So this was the cause of the panic in Morganton!

Indeed.

Now we must leave...

Robur and his men continued working on the machine, which obviously needed considerable repair.

took an interest in studying the mental state of Robur. Had he begun to think of himself as mightier than the elements, even when he possessed just an airship, the *Albatross*?

...and I must insist you remain in your cabin during our journey.

And I am afraid I shall need to lock the hatch this time.

I'm sure you understand, Inspector.

Resistance would have been useless. And what good would it have been to remain within the Great Eyrie, whose walls I could not climb?

CLANK!

I understand, Robur. And I hope you understand, this is where I stop being along for the ride...

How much more powerful had he become, when earth, air and water offered him an endless field where no one could follow him!

...and start to do my job.

Being an inspector for the federal police, you learn one or two interesting tricks — one of them, how to pick a lock.

KLIK

At first I had the feeling that our craft left the earth. Some swerves and balancings in the air followed.

Then the turbines began to spin with amazing speed, while the great wings beat steadily.

And while I admit, there are many criminals who could do this much faster than me...

...I eventually freed myse and decided to bring thi whole affair to a close.

In the middle of this wild excitement, my passion and instincts of duty arose within me!

ROBUR!

In the name of the law--

Hnh!

Forgetting it was one against three, an that we were in mid-air above a howlin ocean, I leapt towards the stern.

I survived, although I don't know how.

When I awoke, I was on board the steamer *Ottawa*, in the Gulf of Mexico.

This ship, while sailing in the same thunderstorm which had destroyed the *Terror*, had noticed some wreckage. My helpless body was found amongst the remains.

I asked if they had found any other survivors...

The Master of the World had disappeared forever, struck down by the thunderbolts which he had dared to brave.

...but there was no news of Robur and his two accomplices.

Over the next five days, we sailed across peaceful waters, back towards the United States.

He took with him the secret of his extraordinary machine.

With nothing to do but sit and wait, I spent my time watching the circling gulls, birds at home on land, sea or air...

...and wondering if the world had really seen the last of the man who had mastered those elements.

Robur the Conqueror.

The Master of the World.

68

About Us

It is night-time in the forest. The sky is black, studded with countless stars. A campfire is crackling, and the storytelling has begun. Stories about love and wisdom, conflict and power, dreams and identity, courage and adventure, survival against all odds, and hope against all hope – they have all come to the fore in a stream of words, gestures, song and dance. The warm, cheerful radiance of the campfire has awoken the storyteller in all those present. Even the trees and the earth and the animals of the forest seem to have fallen silent, captivated, bewitched.

Inspired by this enduring relationship between a campfire and the stories it evokes, we began publishing under the Campfire imprint in 2008, with the vision of creating graphic novels of the finest quality to entertain and educate our readers. Our writers, editors, artists and colourists share a deep passion for good stories and the art of storytelling, so our books are well researched, beautifully illustrated and wonderfully written to create a most enjoyable reading experience.

Our graphic novels are presently being published in four exciting categories. The *Classics* category showcases popular and timeless literature, which has been faithfully adapted for today's readers. While these adaptations retain the flavour of the era, they encourage our readers to delve into the literary world with the aid of authentic graphics and simplified language. Titles in the *Originals* category feature imaginative new characters and intriguing plots, and will be highly anticipated and appreciated by lovers of fiction. Our *Mythology* titles tap into the vast library of epics, myths, and legends from India and abroad, not just presenting tales from time immemorial, but also addressing their modern-day relevance. And our *Biography* titles explore the life and times of eminent personalities from around the world, in a manner that is both inspirational and personal.

Crafted by a new generation of talented artists and writers, all our graphic novels boast cutting-edge artwork, an engaging narrative, and have universal and lasting appeal.

Whether you are an avid reader or an occasional one, we hope you will gather around our campfire and let us draw you into our fascinating world of storytelling.

Can you imagine a vehicle that can travel on land, over water, underwater, and even in air? Jules Verne conceived of such a machine about a century ago! Isn't it a fantastic idea even now? Here are a few interesting facts about two present-day machines.

What is a Hovercraft?

A **hovercraft** is an air-cushion vehicle, also called a ground-effect machine, which can move on the surface of land as well as water. In a hovercraft, air is forced downwards so that air pressure is created between the vehicle and the ground. This allows the vehicle to remain on the surface.

Propellers: These are used for moving the hovercraft forwards. The speed of the propellers can be altered to change direction.They can be used to provide lift too.

Cabin: The cabin is a compartment used by passengers travelling on the hovercraft. The number of passengers varies in different hovercrafts.

Flight deck: Also called the control cabin, the flight deck is raised above the passenger cabin at the front. This is where the captain and the main crew sit and guide the hovercraft.

Motor: The motor is usually located at the rear of the vehicle. It is the heaviest of the components because of which extra pressure is required under that area, in order to attain hovering capabilities.

Lift fans: These are cylindrical fans that take in air and push it down in order to keep the hovercraft afloat.

Skirt: The skirt is one of the most important parts of a hovercraft, as it allows the vehicle to move over obstacles. It is used to hold the air down so that the hovercraft can travel over a wide range of terrain. It is made of rubber, and is an excellent buffer and hull protector.

Who invented the first hovercraft and how?

In the mid-1870s, Sir John Thornycroft, from Great Britain, was the first man to come up with the idea of a hovercraft. He reasoned that a vehicle could travel both on the surface of water and land, and could even be made to move faster if a boxful of air could be kept under it as a hull. Unfortunately, his experiment failed because the boxful of air (hull) could not be kept stable underwater, and kept getting washed away. It was Sir Christopher Cockerell, another Englishman, who finally succeeded in building a proper hovercraft in 1950.

Which was the world's first hovercraft, and how many people did it carry?

The SR N1 was the world's first full-sized hovercraft. It travelled across the English Channel from Calais to Dover on 25th July 1959, and carried only three people.

What is a Seaplane?

A **seaplane** is a plane which can float on the surface of water, and can also take-off into the air from water and land.

Who made the first seaplanes?
Glenn H Curtiss made and flew the first seaplanes in the USA in 1911-12.

What is a float seaplane?
It is a kind of seaplane with slim pontoons which hold up the main body when they come into contact with the water.

What are flying boats?
Seaplanes that have a hull resembling a boat are called flying boats.

What are the two essential features in a seaplane?
Buoyancy and low water resistance are the two features that are essential to a seaplane.

Wings: The wings hold the plane in the air. They also help to balance the plane by making it bank, tilt and turn. They carry navigation lights, to show which way the plane is travelling.

Tail: The tail usually has a fixed horizontal piece and a fixed vertical piece, which are called stabilisers. The stabilisers' job is to provide balance to the aircraft to ensure that it flies straight. The vertical stabiliser keeps the nose of the plane from swinging from side to side, while the horizontal stabiliser prevents an up-and-down motion.

Propeller: The propeller is a set of rotating blades that push the air backwards and give the plane a thrust. It is turned by the engine.

Pontoons or floats: They help the seaplane to touch down on water and skim along it. Flying boats, however, have sponsons, which are short wing-like projections extending from the sides of the hull.

Fuselage: The fuselage, or body, of the airplane holds all the pieces together. The pilots sit in the cockpit at the front of the fuselage. Passengers and cargo are carried in the rear.

DID YOU KNOW?

Rescue services keep a seaplane at hand, as it can locate and retrieve victims from water. In extremely cold areas it is invaluable, as victims are rescued as soon as they are spotted, rather than having to wait for help to arrive at the site.

CAMPFIRE™